100

HELEN EXLEY GIFTBOOKS:
for the most thoughtful gifts of all

OTHER HELEN EXLEY GIFTBOOKS:

Wisdom for the New Millennium
Thoughts on... Being at Peace
Thoughts on... Being Happy
In Beauty May I Walk
Seize The Day! Enjoy the Moment
Words of Wisdom
Words on Courage
Words on Kindness
Words on Joy

Published simultaneously in 2000 by Exley Publications Ltd in Great Britain,
and Exley Publications LLC in the USA.

2 4 6 8 10 12 11 9 7 5 3

Selection and arrangement copyright © Helen Exley 2000.
The moral right of the author has been asserted.

ISBN 1-86187-113-9

Words and pictures selected by Helen Exley.
Pictures researched by Image Select International.
Printed in China.

Exley Publications Ltd, 16 Chalk Hill, Watford, Herts WD19 4BG, UK.
Exley Publications LLC, 232 Madison Avenue, Suite 1409, NY 10016, USA.

...AND
WISDOM
COMES
QUIETLY

A HELEN EXLEY GIFTBOOK

EXLEY

NEW YORK • WATFORD, UK

WHAT LIFE CAN COMPARE TO THIS?
SITTING QUIETLY BY THE WINDOW,
I WATCH THE LEAVES FALL
AND THE FLOWERS BLOOM,
AS THE SEASONS COME AND GO.

HSUEH-TOU (950-1052)

We need time to dream,
time to remember,
and time to reach the infinite.
Time to be.

GLADYS TABER

(1899-1980)

Let us spend one day as deliberately as nature, and not be thrown off the track by every nutshell and mosquito's wing that falls on the rails. Let us rise early and fast, or break fast, gently and without perturbation.... Let us not be upset and overwhelmed in that terrible rapid and whirlpool.... If the engine whistles, let it whistle till it is hoarse for its pains. If the bell rings, why should we run?

HENRY DAVID THOREAU (1817-1862)

I lay in a meadow
until the unwrinkled serenity
entered into my bones,
and made me into one
with the browsing kine,
the still greenery,
the drifting clouds,
and the swooping birds.

ALICE JAMES (1848-1892)

I expand and live in the warm day
like corn and melons.

RALPH WALDO EMERSON (1803-1882)

ALL MEN'S
MISERIES DERIVE FROM NOT BEING ABLE
TO SIT QUIET
IN A ROOM ALONE.

BLAISE PASCAL (1623-1662)

*...ere is great
...appiness
...ot wanting,
... not being
...omething,
... not going
...omewhere.*

You do not need to leave your room....

Remain sitting at your table and listen.

Do not even listen, simply wait.

Do not even wait, be quite still and solitary.

The world will freely offer itself to you to be unmasked.

It has no choice.

It will roll in ecstasy at your feet.

FRANZ KAFKA (1883-1924)

Knowledge was inherent in all things.
The world was a library and its books
were the stones, leaves, grass, brooks....
We learned to do what only the students
of nature ever learn, and that was to feel beauty.

LUTHER STANDING BEAR (1868-1939)

THE HOURS WHEN THE MIND

IS ABSORBED BY BEAUTY

ARE THE ONLY HOURS WE LIVE.

RICHARD JEFFRIES (1848-1887)

He [the American Indian] believes profoundly
in silence – the sign of a perfect equilibrium.
Silence is the absolute poise or balance of body,
mind and spirit. The man who preserves
his selfhood ever calm and unshaken by the storms
of existence – not a leaf, as it were, astir
on the tree; not a ripple upon the surface of
the shining pool – his, in the mind of
the unlettered sage, is the ideal attitude
and conduct of life.... If you ask:
"What are the fruits of silence?" he will say:
"They are self-control, true courage or
endurance, patience, dignity, and reverence.
Silence is the cornerstone of character."

OHIYESA
(DR. CHARLES EASTMAN),
SANTEE SIOUX

LEAVE HOME IN THE SUNSHINE:

DANCE THROUGH A MEADOW —

OR SIT BY A STREAM AND JUST BE.

THE LILT OF THE WATER

WILL GATHER YOUR WORRIES

AND CARRY THEM DOWN TO THE SEA.

J .   D O N A L D   W A L T E R S

Nothing will content those who

A bag of apples, a pot of homemade jam,
a scribbled note, a bunch of golden flowers,
a coloured pebble, a box of seedlings,
an empty scent bottle for the children....
Who needs diamonds and van-delivered bouquets?

PAM BROWN, b.1928

LESS IS MORE.

ROBERT BROWNING (1812-1889)

are not content with a little.

G R E E K   P R O V E R B

You can't have everything

Where would you put it?

ANN LANDERS, b. 1918

THE
MORNING
SUN,
THE
NEW
SWEET
EARTH
AND
THE
GREAT
SILENCE.

T.C. McLUHAN

When I am alone
the flowers are really seen;
I can pay attention
to them.
They are felt presences.

MAY SARTON (1912-1995)

For the past eighty years I have started each day in the same manner. It is not a mechanical routine but something essential to my daily life. I go to the piano, and play two preludes and fugues of Bach. I cannot think of doing otherwise. It is a sort of benediction on the house. But that is not its only meaning for me. It is a rediscovery of the world of which I have the joy of being a part. It fills me with awareness of the wonder of life, with a feeling of the incredible marvel of being a human being.

PABLO CASALS (1876-1973)

One cannot collect
all the beautiful shells
on the beach.
One can collect
only a few,
and they are more
beautiful if they
are few.

ANNE MORROW LINDBERGH, b.1906,
FROM "GIFT FROM THE SEA"

THE MIRACLE IS NOT TO FLY IN THE AIR, OR TO WALK ON THE WATER, BUT TO WALK ON THE EARTH.

CHINESE PROVERB

It is good to be alone

in a garden at dawn or dark

so that all its shy presences

may haunt you and possess you

in a reverie of suspended thought.

JAMES DOUGLAS

... a reverie of suspended thought

... THOSE WHO KNOW

THE VALUE

AND THE EXQUISITE TASTE

OF SOLITARY FREEDOM

(FOR ONE IS ONLY FREE

WHEN ONE IS ALONE)....

ISABELLE EBERHARDT (1877-1904)

WHAT A LOVELY SURPRISE
TO DISCOVER HOW UN-LONELY
BEING ALONE CAN BE.

ELLEN BURSTYN, b. 1932

GENTLENESS is everywhere in daily life, a sign that faith rules through

ordinary things: through cooking and small talk, through storytelling,

making love, fishing, tending animals and sweetcorn and flowers, through

sports, music and books, raising kids – all the places where the gravy soaks in

and grace shines through. Even in a time of elephantine vanity and greed,

one never has to look far to see the campfires of gentle people.

GARRISON KEILLOR, b.1942

p e o p l e

In this world there is nothing softer
or thinner than water.
But to compel the hard and unyielding,
it has no equal.
That the weak overcomes the strong,
that the hard gives way to the gentle —
This everyone knows,
yet no one acts accordingly.

LAO-TZU (6TH CENTURY B.C.)

WEAK

HE WHO SMILES RATHER THAN RAGES IS ALWAYS THE STRONGER.

JAPANESE WISDOM

STRONG

Contentment...
comes as the infallible result
of great acceptances,
great humilities –
of not trying to make ourselves
this or that
(to conform to some dramatized
version of ourselves),
but of surrendering ourselves
to the fullness of life –
of letting life
flow through us.

DAVID GRAYSON

THE WAY TO USE LIFE
IS TO DO NOTHING
THROUGH ACTING,
THE WAY TO USE LIFE
IS TO DO EVERYTHING
THROUGH BEING.

LAO-TZU (6TH CENTURY B.C.)

*Our greatest experiences
are our quietest moments.*

NIETZSCHE (1844-1900)

Look for a lovely thing
and you will find it,
It is not far —
It never will be far.

SARA TEASDALE

Nature is painting for us,
day after day,
pictures of infinite beauty
if only we have eyes
to see them....

JOHN RUSKIN (1819-1900)

ARRANGING

A BOWL OF FLOWERS

IN THE MORNING

CAN GIVE A SENSE OF QUIET

IN A CROWDED DAY —

LIKE WRITING A POEM,

OR SAYING A PRAYER.

ANNE MORROW LINDBERGH, b.1906

Come away from the din.

Come away to the quiet fields,

over which the great sky stretches,

and where, between us and the stars,

there lies but silence;

and there, in the stillness

let us listen to the voice

that is speaking within us.

JEROME K. JEROME (1859-1927)

Our language has wisely
sensed the two sides
of being alone. It has created
the word "loneliness"
to express the pain of being alone.
And it has created the word
"solitude" to express
the glory of being alone.

PAUL TILLICH (1886-1965)

IF ONLY
I MAY GROW:
FIRMER,
SIMPLER –
QUIETER,
WARMER.

DAG HAMMARSKJÖLD
(1905-1961)

Do we need to make a special effort to enjoy the beauty of the blue sky?

Do we have to practice to be able to enjoy it? No, we just enjoy it.

Each second, each minute of our lives can be like this.

Wherever we are, any time, we have the capacity to enjoy the sunshine,

the presence of each other, even the sensation of our breathing.

We don't need to go to China to enjoy the blue sky.

We don't have to travel into the future to enjoy our breathing.

We can be in touch with these things right now.

THICH NHAT HANH, b.1926

Do not let trifles disturb your tranquillity of mind....
Life is too precious to be sacrificed for the nonessential
and transient.... Ignore the inconsequential.

GRENVILLE KLEISER (1868-1953)

*There is no quiet place
in the white man's cities,
no place to hear the leaves of spring
or the rustle of insect's wings....
The Indians prefer the soft sound of
the wind darting over the face of the pond,
the smell of the wind itself cleansed
by the midday rain,
or scented with pinion pine.*

CHIEF SEATTLE (1786 - 1866)

Listen in deep silence.
Be very still and open your mind....
Sink deep into the peace
that waits for you beyond the frantic,
riotous thoughts and sights
and sounds of this insane world.

FROM "A COURSE IN MIRACLES"

silence

LET MY DOING NOTHING
WHEN I HAVE NOTHING TO DO
BECOME UNTROUBLED IN ITS DEPTH
OF PEACE LIKE THE EVENING IN THE SEASHORE
WHEN THE WATER IS SILENT.

RABINDRANATH TAGORE (1861-1941)

To be without some of the things you want is an indispensable part of happiness.

BERTRAND RUSSELL

(1872-1970)

The strong, calm person
is always loved and revered.
He is like a shade-giving tree
in a thirsty land,
or a sheltering rock in a storm.

JAMES ALLEN (1864-1912)

FROM SERENITY COMES GENTLENESS, COMES LASTING STRENGTH.

PAM BROWN, b.1928

To a mind that is still
the whole universe surrenders.

CHUANG TZU (369-286 B.C.)

Better than a thousand
useless words
is one single word that
gives peace.

THE DHAMMAPADA

Over all the mountaintops
Is peace.
In all treetops
You perceive
Scarcely a breath.
The little birds in the forest
Are silent.
Wait then; soon
You, too, will have peace.

JOHANN WOLFGANG VON GOETHE (1749-1832)

My greatest wealth is the deep stillness
in which I strive and grow
and win what the world cannot take
from me with fire or sword.

JOHANN WOLFGANG VON GOETHE
(1749-1832)

THE POOR
LONG FOR RICHES
AND THE RICH FOR HEAVEN,
BUT THE WISE
LONG FOR A STATE OF
TRANQUILLITY.

SWAMI RAMA (1873-1906)

The quiet mind is richer than a crown....

Such sweet content, such minds, such sleep, such bliss

Beggars enjoy when princes oft do miss.

ROBERT GREENE (1558-1592)

Ultimately we have just one moral duty:
to reclaim large areas of peace in ourselves,
more and more peace,
and to reflect it toward others.
And the more peace there is in us,
the more peace there will be in our troubled world.

ETTY HILLESUM (1914-1943)

PEACE IS INEVITABLE TO THOSE WHO OFFER PEACE.

FROM "A COURSE IN MIRACLES"

CE

Countries like ours are full of people who have all of the material comforts they desire, yet lead lives of quiet (and at times noisy) desperation, understanding nothing but the fact that there is a hole inside them and that however much food and drink they pour into it, however many motorcars and television sets they stuff it with, however many well-balanced children and loyal friends they parade around the edges of it... it aches!

BERNARD LEVIN, b.1928

Do nondoing,

strive for nonstriving,

savour the flavourless,

regard the small as important,

make much of little,

repay enmity with virtue;

plan for difficulty

when it is still easy,

do the great

while it is still small.

LAO-TZU (6TH CENTURY B.C.)

WE ARE INVOLVED

IN A LIFE

THAT PASSES UNDERSTANDING

AND OUR HIGHEST BUSINESS

IS OUR DAILY LIFE.

JOHN CAGE (1912-1992), FROM
"WHERE ARE WE GOING
AND WHAT ARE WE DOING?"

Days tumbled on days,
I was in my overalls,
didn't comb my hair,
didn't shave much,
consorted only with dogs and cats,
I was living the happy life
of childhood again....
I was as nutty as a fruitcake
and happier. Sunday afternoon,
then, I'd go to my woods
with the dogs and sit
and put out my hands
palms up and accept handfuls
of sun boiling over the palms.

JACK KEROUAC (1922-1969), FROM "THE DHARMA BUMS"

I hope you find joy in the great things of life —
but also in the little things. A flower, a song, a butterfly
on your hand.

ELLEN LEVINE

I have learned
to have very modest goals
for society and myself;
things like clean air, green grass,
children with bright eyes,
not being pushed around,
useful work that suits one's abilities,
plain tasty food,
and occasional satisfying nookie.

PAUL GOODMAN (1911-1972)

There are so few... empty hours in the day, or

empty rooms in my life in which to stand

alone and find myself. Too many activities, and

people, and things, and interesting people.

For it is not merely the trivial which clutters

our lives but the important as well.

We can have a surfeit of treasures....

ANNE MORROW LINDBERGH, b.1906, FROM "GIFT FROM THE SEA"

THE CURE FOR ALL THE ILLNESS OF LIFE
IS STORED IN THE INNER DEPTH OF LIFE ITSELF,
THE ACCESS TO WHICH BECOMES POSSIBLE
WHEN WE ARE ALONE.
THIS SOLITUDE IS A WORLD IN ITSELF,
FULL OF WONDERS AND RESOURCES
UNTHOUGHT OF.
IT IS ABSURDLY NEAR; YET
SO UNAPPROACHABLY DISTANT.

RABINDRANATH TAGORE (1861-1941)

TRUE BEAUTY MUST COME, MUST BE GROWN, FROM WITHIN....

RALPH W. TRINE (1866-1958)

When we experience moments of ecstasy —
in play, in art, in sex — they come not as
an exception, an accident, but as a taste of what
life is meant to be.... Ecstasy is an idea, a goal,
but it can be the expectation of every day.
Those times when we're grounded in our body,
pure in our heart, clear in our mind, rooted
in our soul, and suffused with the energy,
the spirit of life, are our birthright.
It's really not that hard to stop and luxuriate
in the joy and wonder of being.
Children do it all the time.
It's a natural human gift that should be
at the heart of our lives.

GABRIELLE ROTH

You ask

why I make my home

in the mountain forest,

and I smile,

and am silent,

and even my soul

remains quiet;

it lives

in the other world

which no one owns.

The peach trees blossom.

The water flows.

LI PO (701-762)

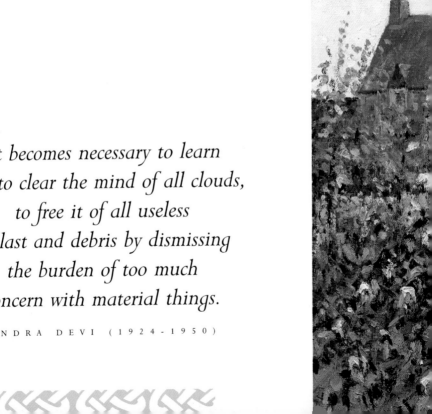

It becomes necessary to learn
how to clear the mind of all clouds,
to free it of all useless
ballast and debris by dismissing
the burden of too much
concern with material things.

INDRA DEVI (1924-1950)

*Let your boat of life
be light, packed only with what you need —
a homely home and simple pleasures,
one or two friends worth
the name, someone to love and to love you, a cat,
a dog, enough to eat and enough to wear....*

JEROME K. JEROME (1859-1927)

HE IS HAPPIEST,
BE HE KING
OR PEASANT,
WHO FINDS PEACE
IN HIS HOME.

JOHANN WOLFGANG VON GOETHE (1749-1832)

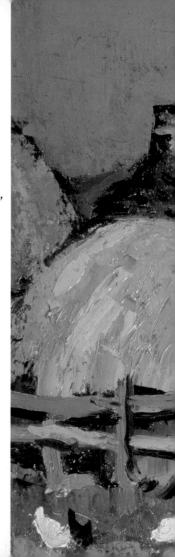

Property is not essential.
But happiness,
a love of beauty,
friendship between all peoples
and individuals,
is life itself.

LAURIE STOCKWELL

POOR AND CONTENT IS RICH, AND RICH ENOUGH.

WILLIAM SHAKESPEARE (1564-1616)

How simple and frugal
a thing is happiness: a glass of wine,
a roast chestnut, a wretched little brazier,
the sound of the sea....
All that is required to feel that here and now
is happiness, is a simple, frugal heart.

NIKOS KAZANTZAKIS (1883-1957)

h u m

s i m p l e

HE OR SHE WHO KNOWS
THAT ENOUGH IS ENOUGH
WILL ALWAYS HAVE ENOUGH.

LAO-TZU (6TH CENTURY B.C.)

To be content
with what we possess
is the greatest
and most secure of riches.

MARCUS TULLIUS CICERO
(106-43 B.C.)

*My earliest emotions
are bound to the earth
and to the labors of the fields.
I find in the land
a profound suggestion of poverty
and I love poverty above all other things;
not sordid and famished poverty
but poverty that is blessed — simple,
humble, like brown bread.*

FEDERICO GARCÍA LORCA
(1898-1936)

The tipi is much better to live in; always clean, warm in winter, cool in summer; easy to move. The white man builds big house, cost much money, like big cage, shut out sun, can never move; always sick.

CHIEF FLYING HAWK (1852-1931)

In solitude,
where we are least alone.

LORD BYRON (1788-1824)

*Loneliness
is the poverty of self,
solitude
is the richness of self.*

MAY SARTON (1912-1995)

Above all, let us never forget
that an act of goodness
is in itself an act of happiness.
It is the flower of a long inner life
of joy and contentment;
it tells of peaceful hours and days
on the sunniest heights
of our soul.

COUNT MAURICE MAETERLINCK (1862-1949)

TRUE JOY IS SERENE.

SENECA (c.4 B.C.-65 A.D.)

I do not want to change.
I want the same old
and loved things, the same
trees and soft ashgreen;
the turtle-doves,
the blackbirds, the coloured
yellow-hammer sing, sing,
singing so long as there is
light to cast a shadow
on the dial, for such is
the measure of his song,
and I want them
in the same place.

RICHARD JEFFRIES (1848-1887)

Simplify. Stop bothering
with the non-essentials.
Having devoted my life
to my work so far,
I should reap the harvest
and learn how to live
the rest of it properly.
It's time now for trees
and grass and
growing things.

AUTHOR UNKNOWN

Drinking tea,

eating rice,

I pass my time

as it comes;

Looking down at

the stream,

Looking up at

the mountain,

How serene

and relaxed

I feel indeed!

PAO-TZU WEN-CH'I (c.900)

There is in all things

an inexhaustible sweetness

and purity,

a silence that is a fountain

of action and joy.

It rises up in wordless gentleness

and flows out of me

from unseen roots

of all created being.

THOMAS MERTON (1915-1968)

Never be afraid
to sit awhile
and think.

LORRAINE HANSBERRY (1930-1965)

SITTING SILENTLY,
DOING NOTHING,
SPRING COMES,
AND THE GRASS GROWS
BY ITSELF.

OSHO (1931-1990)

Here will we sit
and let the sounds of music
creep in our ears:
soft stillness and the night
become the touches of
sweet harmony.

WILLIAM SHAKESPEARE
(1564-1616)

THE QUIETER YOU BECOME, THE MORE YOU CAN HEAR.

BABA RAM DASS

AND SO, WHILE OTHERS

MISERABLY PLEDGE THEMSELVES

TO THE PURSUIT OF AMBITION

AND BRIEF POWER,

I WILL BE STRETCHED OUT IN THE SHADE,

SINGING.

FRAY LUIS DE LEÓN (c.1527-1591)

I asked for riches that I might be happy;
I was given poverty that I might be wise.

I asked for all things that I might enjoy life;
I was given life that I might enjoy all things.

I was given nothing that I asked for;
But everything that I had hoped for.

PEACE
IS THE FAIREST FORM
OF HAPPINESS.

WILLIAM ELLERY CHANNING (1780-1842)

Though we travel the world over
to find the beautiful,
we must carry it with us
or we find it not.

RALPH WALDO EMERSON (1803-1882)

Deep in the soul, below pain,
below all the distraction of life,
is a silence vast and grand — an infinite ocean
of calm, which nothing can disturb;
nature's own exceeding peace,
which "passes understanding".
That which we seek with passionate longing,
here and there, upward and outward;
we find at last within ourselves.

C . M . C .   Q U O T E D   B Y   R . M .   B U C K E

There is a silence into which the world cannot intrude.
There is an ancient peace
you carry in your heart and have not lost.

FROM "A COURSE IN MIRACLES"

LIFE IS EATING US UP.
WE SHALL BE FABLES PRESENTLY.
KEEP COOL: IT WILL BE ALL ONE
A HUNDRED YEARS HENCE.

RALPH WALDO EMERSON (1803-1882)

*M*ay peace and peace
and peace be everywhere.

THE UPANISHADS
(c.900-600 B.C.)

ACKNOWLEDGEMENTS
The publishers are grateful for permission to reproduce copyright material. Whilst every reasonable effort has been made to trace copyright holders, the publishers would be pleased to hear from any not here acknowledged. JACK KEROUAC: From *The Dharma Bums*, published by Penguin Books © 1958 Jack Kerouac, renewed 1986 Stella Kerouac and Jan Kerouac. BERNARD LEVIN: From Times Newspapers Ltd. © Bernard Levin 1968. GABRIELLE ROTH: From *Maps to Ecstasy* © 1989 New World Library, Novato, CA. SARA TEASDALE: From "Night" reprinted with permission of Simon and Schuster from *The Collected Poems of Sara Teasdale* © 1930 Sara Teasdale Filsinger; copyright renewed © 1958 by Guaranty Trust Company of New York, Executor. J. DONALD WALTERS: From *There's Joy in the Heavens* published by Crystal Clarity Publishers.

LIST OF ILLUSTRATIONS
Exley Publications is very grateful to the following individuals and organizations for permission to reproduce their pictures. Whilst all reasonable efforts have been made to clear copyright and acknowledge sources and artists, Exley Publications would be happy to hear from any copyright holder who may have been omitted.

Cover, title page and endpapers: *Winter Sun*, © 2000 MAX CLARENBACH, Galerie Paffrath

Page 6: *View from a Window*, SPENCER FREDERICK GORE, Southampton City Art Gallery, The Bridgeman Art Library

Pages 8/9: *View over the Churn Valley, Upper Coberley, Gloucestershire*, © 2000 CHARLES NEAL, SuperStock

Page 11: *Still Life of a Kettle*, PAUL CÉZANNE, Musée D'Orsay, Paris, AISA

Pages 12/13: *River Nene, Near Widenhoe, Northamptonshire*, © 2000 CHARLES NEAL, SuperStock

Page 15: *The Breakfast Table*, © 2000 JOSEPH MILNER KITE, Waterhouse and Dodd, London, The Bridgeman Art Library

Pages 16/17: *November Moon*, © 2000 JULIAN NOVOROL, The Bridgeman Art Library

Page 19: © 2000 PETER FIORE, Artworks

Page 20: *The River*, © 2000 YVONNE DELVO, The Bridgeman Art Library

Pages 22/23: *Normandy Farm, Summer*, PAUL CÉZANNE, AKG

Pages 24/25: *Water and Stones*, © 2000 ALEKSANDR ANDREEVIC IVANOV, Russian State Museum, St. Petersburg, SuperStock

Page 27: *Still Life*, PAUL CÉZANNE, Private Collection

Pages 28/29: *A Herbaceous Border*, © 2000 HUGH L. NORRIS, Christopher Wood Gallery, London, The Bridgeman Art Library

Pages 30/31: *Woodmancote, Gloucestershire*, © 2000 CHARLES NEAL, SuperStock

Page 33: *St. Tropez Flowers*, © 2000 RICHARD CARLINE, Edimedia

Page 34: *Rock Lily*, © 2000 MARGARET PRESTON, Australian National Gallery, Canberra, The Bridgeman Art Library

Page 37: *Natura Morta con ramo dimeol*, © 2000 KUZMA PETROV-VODKIN, Scala

Page 38: *May Petals on the Moat Edge*, © 2000 TIMOTHY EASTON, The Bridgeman Art Library

Pages 40/41: *Twilight near Albany*, GEORGE H. BOUGHTON, Private Collection

Page 43: Artist Unknown, Chris Beetles Gallery

Page 45: *Children and young girls picking flowers in a meadow north of Skagen*, MICHAEL PETER ANCHER, Skagens Museum, Denmark, The Bridgeman Art Library

Pages 46/47: *Winter in Wittever*, © 2000 MAX CLARENBACH, Galerie Paffrath

Page 49: *Through a Window*, © 2000 WALTER FARMER, The Bridgeman Art Library

Pages 50/51: *Sunset and fog at Eragny*, CAMILLE PISSARRO, SuperStock

Pages 52/53: *Dappled Light on the Iris Field*, © 2000 TIMOTHY EASTON, The Bridgeman Art Library

Page 55: *Agapanthus Molucela*, © 2000 KAREN ARMITAGE, The Bridgeman Art Library

Pages 56/57: *Stormy Sunset*, JOHN RUSKIN, Ruskin Museum, Coniston, The Bridgeman Art Library

Pages 58/59: *Ripe Wheatfields*, FRITZ OVERBECK, Worpsweder Kunsthalle, Stade, The Bridgeman Art Library

Pages 60/61: *Reflections in a Norwegian Fjord*, ADELSTEEN NORMANN, Fine Art Photographic Library